Praise for *What Can the Matter Be?*

"In *What Can the Matter Be?*, Michigan's beloved Keith Taylor explores our inland seas' ecosystems, as well as family history and lore, in order 'to prove some things last.' Whether from Isle Royale, his 'wild backyard,' or the 'beautifully indifferent' trees, the wit and wonder of Taylor's essential, intimate poems resist 'Extinction Report[s]' and sustain us."

—Terry Bohnhorst Blackhawk, author of
One Less River and *Maumee, Maumee*

"Keith Taylor brings a birder's eye to the everyday, and a birder's ear to what stands out in the silence of what is luminous about the particulars of a life well-lived by paying attention. 'We are made of this,' Taylor tells us. 'Remember this.' Taylor is often astonished by both the beauty of the ordinary world and the inevitable realization that, 'I cannot believe our world is dying.' And yet here in this book the act of looking and listening is a way for us to honor our time here, and 'to prove some things last' and that 'We are quiet here / and think we might stay a while.' These are poems that remind us that 'Still, light rises' 'and in that moment your whole world glows.'"

—Peter Markus, author of *When Our Fathers Return to Us as Birds* (Wayne State University Press)

"*What Can the Matter Be?* is a graceful but also urgent meditation on birds, botany, and humanity. In wide-ranging forms—from very short poems to micro essays—Taylor shares the pleasures of a life spent noticing. Here you'll find piping plovers, watercress, moss, owls, herons, monarchs, salamanders, flycatchers, and prairie warblers. You'll also find stumps, fences, sidewalks, and colossal wildfires. Whether he is thinking about what we have lost or what splendor remains, Keith Taylor summons language of wit and tenderness to ponder our natural world. This is a book of observation, celebration, lament, and delight. It is proof, as Taylor writes, that 'some things last.'"

—Cindy Hunter Morgan, author of *Harborless* and
Far Company (both Wayne State University Press)

"This stunning hybrid collection of poems and lyric essays carries Taylor's signature precision coupled with the subtle nuances of an observer who always sees under the surface to the plain truth of things. Here, his wisdom in abundance—a perfectly balanced literary restraint that creates those quiet insights that still leap and often ring with irony. From the singular chair at the window to communal environmental grief, from backyard to international settings, these pieces invite our engagement, the pleasure of saying, *Oh yes, I see it too*. Thank you, Keith Taylor, for being true, for not fully explaining the mystery, for writing what happens if we let it be, if we let it touch us."
—Anne-Marie Oomen, 2023–24 Michigan Author Award recipient
and author of *As Long as I Know You: The Mom Book*

"In this difficult time, Keith Taylor finds connections, not borders. Using subtle brushstrokes, he scrutinizes the balances and imbalances of the natural world and the human with both reverence and humor. We can all learn from these brilliant poems. We too must honor the world, look at it as closely ourselves."
—Jim Daniels, author of *Comment Card* and
Gun/Shy (Wayne State University Press)

WHAT CAN THE MATTER BE?

Made in Michigan Writers Series

GENERAL EDITORS

Michael Delp, Interlochen Center for the Arts
M. L. Liebler, Wayne State University

A complete listing of the books in this series can be
found online at wsupress.wayne.edu.

WHAT CAN THE MATTER BE?

POEMS BY
KEITH TAYLOR

WAYNE STATE UNIVERSITY PRESS
DETROIT

ISBN 9780814351406 (paperback)
ISBN 9780814351413 (e-book)

Library of Congress Control Number: 2024930769

Cover art courtesy of the Biodiversity Heritage Library / Smithsonian and the New York Public Library. Cover design by Shoshana Schultz.

Publication of this book was made possible by a generous gift from The Meijer Foundation.

Wayne State University Press rests on Waawiyaataanong, also referred to as Detroit, the ancestral and contemporary homeland of the Three Fires Confederacy. These sovereign lands were granted by the Ojibwe, Odawa, Potawatomi, and Wyandot Nations, in 1807, through the Treaty of Detroit. Wayne State University Press affirms Indigenous sovereignty and honors all tribes with a connection to Detroit. With our Native neighbors, the press works to advance educational equity and promote a better future for the earth and all people.

Wayne State University Press
Leonard N. Simons Building
4809 Woodward Avenue
Detroit, Michigan 48201-1309

Visit us online at wsupress.wayne.edu.

For Stephen Leggett,
old friend

CONTENTS

1. The Extinction Report

2. The Longing for Home

3. Some Things Last

4. Botanists in Love

1

THE EXTINCTION REPORT

Johnny's Too Long at the Fair

Oh, dear,
what can the matter be

I haven't been
outside in months.

From the window
I watch chipmunks

piling up dirt
from the holes

they've dug
through the yard.

At night I see
the shadows of foxes

and coyotes slink
into the back lot.

Raccoons growl and howl
outside my door.

Oh, dear,
what can the matter be

I haven't seen any cars
on the street for days,

just thin young people
running,

wearing bright,
tight clothes,

hats pulled down
to their eyebrows

and masks up
past their noses.

Oh, dear,
what can the matter be

My neighbor left
a note on the door

saying—people
are marching

on Main Street,
carrying signs

and dancing
across the yellow lines!

I keep watch
in my window

but they haven't
come by here, yet.

Oh, dear,
what can the matter be?

When the Beast Passes Through

Woke to snow light
in our last significant snow

on a quiet day
in a time of quiet days

and tracks in the snow
up from the avenue

fresh tracks
very fresh

canid tracks
but no dog

walks like this
in a straight line

one foot directly
before the last

up and out
toward our neighbors

Learning to Live with Our Neighbor's New Fence

We hope our new neighbors didn't build
their fence because we did something wrong.

Maybe they just want to keep their dog in
or be comfortably naked in their hot tub.

It's possible they don't like the look of our wild backyard,
unraked for the sake of bugs and butterflies.

Maybe they get worried when I walk out there
in every season wearing binoculars, watching for migrants.

They haven't lived here long enough to see the ash
and mulberry trees come down under snow or ice.

They don't know that our black walnuts and cherries
could drop a limb in any reasonable wind.

The trees might turn their fence to kindling
and there's no way we're paying to fix it.

They won't smell our compost when we move it
closer to their wooden wall (we're good with odor).

They probably won't expect the vines
we'll plant or the elves and fairies

of rot we'll encourage, spreading
slowly into their back corner.

Out of the Attic

I don't mind it *in* the attic,

hearing it scurry above me at night
or seeing it sneak out of the cracks in the roof

when I'm sitting outside,
then watching it fly

like some crazed and jerky swallow
between the oaks.

But this one came *out* of the attic.
Upstairs! In our house!

Now it's flying around my study
dipping behind the books on the top shelves—

my boxed Dickinson,
my two-volume hardcover Williams *Collected*—

making its ugly little sounds
like a bald mouse with sharp teeth.

I have no idea how to get it back in.

The Things We Do

We've done real work,
spent real money to drain

the water away from the foundation
and keep our basement dry.

We send it to the street
or run it underground

so it can filter
down to the aquifer.

We haven't stopped for years,
decades now, and still

I check almost daily
for thin streams running

across the floor
toward my books

or into the closet
where we keep our winter coats.

In the Study

He spends more time in his reading chair
than at his desk. Truth told, he spends
most time in that chair, before the window,
looking out at the backyard drama.

He's seen the hawk that eats small birds
fly in just before the slightly larger hawk
that eats small mammals. Watching them
makes it easy enough to kill an afternoon.

He watches his wife gardening, smiling sometimes.
She looks happy, and he wonders if she would be
happier still if a lifetime ago
she had married a different man.

A Cold Day in April

Chances get better every day
that when I come to die it will
happen in this chair, before this window.

It might even happen on a day
in April, a cold day after weeks
of warmth that brought out blossoms

on the redbud and enough flowers
on the serviceberry to shield
the view of this corpse
from my neighbors to the west.

The day will have rain clouds
moving through quickly, leaving
behind just a few drops to catch
the occasional ray of light
that breaks through the dark.

First leaves, just emerging,
have their moment to flash
shimmering temporary diamonds
before the next cloud and the next gust
turn everything dull gray again.

Tall Oaks

We've lived here only forty years.
The tall oaks have grown old
and started falling. Three came down
in wind and the leaves of two more
grew in thin, a light green,
almost yellow in midsummer.
We had them cut. There was a stump,
three feet across when we moved here.
It rotted for a couple of decades
until only a depression in the garden
was left, looking like a metaphor
for something we didn't understand.

Hermit Stories

I could take you there, down a two-track
barely visible from a back road, to that place
where four old white pines grow above the aspens.
If I took you, we'd cut through bracken
and some scrubby hemlock. I'd make
you find the foundation lines that look
like mounds of moss deep in shade at first,
until you realize they are the only straight
lines in the forest. You might start to see
the house, a small rectangle with a hole
in the middle where he'd keep his food
in the winter. An old Odawa man, who, before
the First War, had been burned out
of his farm at Colonial Point so they
could sell lakeside lots to Chicago money,
told another man beside him in a ward
at the Cheboygan hospital that the hermit
came from California after he'd killed
someone who insulted his wife. The Odawa man
was amused that the hermit had to leave
her then and come two thousand miles
to those pines and our snow. When he died
the woman came to the service the priest
in Brutus insisted on. She was, of course, beautiful.
I've also heard he was a teacher from Grand Rapids.
Under the leaf litter I've found rusty lids
from canning jars and one crushed pail,
its bottom long gone. I once imagined them
at home with my collections of stones
and pine cones, but they make a better story
there, almost hidden in the moss and leaves.
If I took you, I'd ask you not to touch.

In Memory

Dan Minock

Great horned owls have not returned
to the heron rookery, sixteen clumps
of sticks woven high into the oaks
on a small island in a small lake.
For three decades my friend counted
the owls nesting there until herons
returned in spring to claim their place.

My friend can't remember the lake,
its oaks, its herons, or its owls,
so I return midwinter, crunching
over the ice to check for owl-sign.
For five years now, the January nests
have held nothing but snow.

Anecdotal Evidence

Where are the snows of yesteryear?

It comes down heavy,
wet and sloppy, barely
sticking to sidewalks,
roofs, or driveways.
We still buy shovels
for show, in memory
of piles we once had—
crisp, light snow
pushed by any wind
up to window height.
It blocked our doors.
When we walked out,
it crunched beneath our boots,
screaming back at us.
It lasted for months.

The Cull

The city wants to cull the herd—
too many gardens are losing
dogwoods and redbuds
clipped to the ground over winter.

The white-tailed deer have retraced
their snowy trails through our yards,
sneaking in at night to do their work.
We catch only a quick glimpse

when they run off at dawn.
We hear them snort in the dark, not sure
if the sound rises from our dreams.
The city plans to give the meat away.

The Last Monarch

Suddenly there was a summer
without monarchs.

I had seen monarchs
clustered in small trees
on the north shores of large lakes
waiting for a night breeze
to carry them across,
so many butterflies on one tree
that it bent almost to the ground.

And then a summer
without monarchs.

And I had walked one September
beside another lake littered
with the broken orange wings
of monarchs caught in storms
trying to cross.

And just the October before
I'd seen one monarch
lonely on a baseball field,
flying south.

But still . . .
suddenly, one summer
without monarchs . . .

and then
the fall.

Canadian Fires

The moon is red
tonight

and there's a tang
of pine smoke in the air

from fires out West
two thousand miles away

or maybe from those
in northern Quebec

although our winds
don't usually blow
from that direction.

One Species of Greatest Concern

for Amy Schrank

Mudpuppy,
neotenous salamander.

Jesus, who knew? Here
the whole time!

Ugly, and slimy
under rocks or old logs.

Hard to love.
Nocturnal.

This is why
we keep paying attention.

Lidless eyes, gills, a reptilian
fetus stopped halfway.

We find them when, dead,
they float up

close to the beach
where our children play.

Emergency Room

I didn't know the girl.

Her exquisite nurse
        in purple clothes,
        wearing gold earrings
said
        call to her.

I did
        but faintly
        my voice frail and high.

The girl's head
        was turned toward me.

Her eyes—
            such large dark eyes!—
        half opened,
        stared the way dead eyes stare.

Keep breathing!
        the nurse in purple
        screamed,
        shattering the ER.

I backed out of the room
        as if leaving royalty,
        in deference.

Almost Storm

On a warm afternoon I doze off
then awake to the almost storm,
sky gone black, breeze turned to wind,
temperature falling. Little yellow jackets
have given up all thought of stinging
for the duration and take refuge
on the leeward side of my legs.
Lightning strikes straight into the forest
across the lake, its thunder rolling
like irony across this rainless land.

At the End of Empire

My love leans back
in her garden chair,
smiling. She's looking up
things on her phone,
the names of pests
or planting instructions
for early summer.
She might be finishing
the *Times* crossword puzzle.
First there's bird song,
then sirens squawk
from the streets around her.
A squirrel sneaks over
and sleeps for a moment
in the shade she casts.

Responsibilities

I keep the feeders
filled with seeds
so jays come down
noisy and unforgiving.
They chase off
starlings then build
their nests out back.
I watch them
from my study
while far away
towers fall
and ancient cities crumble.

2

THE LONGING FOR HOME

Parthenon Marbles

I shouldn't have taken it,

particularly just to sit
like a neglected trophy
on the ledge in my study
between a piece of copper
I bought in the Keweenaw
and some dead coral shaped like
the Venus of Willendorf
I dove for in the ocean
on the windy and wild side
of Oahu twenty years
before I visited Greece.

I should have left it beside
the new, paved road bisecting
the Acropolis of Rhodes,
mixed in with construction junk,
cement, and broken shoes.

Not the Parthenon Marbles
getting dusty in Bloomsbury—

just my two-inch shard of red clay
with a distinct, delicate
rounded ridge hand-formed and fired
thirty or three thousand years ago
for someone needing
a pot to carry water
or wheat up to the temple—

still, I should have left it there.

Aegina: After School

She was six or seven and was the last child off the bus. She kicked her way through the pines and across the cracked marble.

We paid her father twenty-five drachmas for admission to the grounds. We had taken a boat out from Piraeus that morning, then caught a bus up the mountain to the Temple of Aphaia, a local goddess lost in forest or sea. We came for the pines and view and wind through the double colonnade. But we sat in the shade to watch the child—tiny, and ignoring the out of season tourists:

> Black-haired child kicking
> > stones across the temple yard,
> bored by the last
> > three tourists in November.

The Sickness That Comes from the Longing for Home

1.

When I was well into middle age, I decided I should learn modern
Greek. I had several teachers, all very good, all excited about the histories
of Greek words. My last teacher knew the nuances of American English
and of our popular culture despite a lingering Greek accent. Still, he was
the first to admit gaps in his knowledge. In one lesson, he got excited about
nostalgia.

"*Nostos*," he said. "The return to the home. The longing to return home.
The thing that motivated Odysseus through all those years of war and exile,
past all those barriers thrown up by the gods. And *algos*, pain or sickness.
Not quite the same word as the root for *allergy*, but you get the point.
Nostalgia, then, is *the sickness that comes from the longing for home*. What a
beautiful word! It describes an essential emotion like no other word I know."

"But," I interrupted, "for us the word *nostalgia* has taken on pejorative
connotations. You know, a kind of sloppy sentimentality about a past that
never existed."

"*Nostalgia!* Sloppy sentimentality! Never! It is the sickness that comes
from the longing for home!"

"Nonetheless," I said, "it is not a word we use seriously very much, at
least not about a genuine emotion."

"But what," he said, and he looked more hurt than puzzled, "what then
do you call the sickness that comes from the longing for home?"

2.

Over fifty years ago, when I was living my bohemian years hitchhiking
through Great Britain, Ireland, and France, finding work wherever I could
and accepting it gladly for food and lodging, sleeping in barns, ditches,
youth hostels, or in caves down along the Mediterranean, I would play a little
game with the freaks and hippies I found myself staying with. A few of them
were North Americans, but most were from Western Europe or Australia.
Occasionally there would be a wanderer from Czechoslovakia, Japan, or Korea.

Every one of these young people, all of us languidly searching for the
fringe, seemed to share some version of one bit of folk wisdom, no matter
what our mother tongue: *a rolling stone gathers no moss*. But we seemed to
understand it in radically different ways.

Those differences may no longer exist. It was a long time ago. Now, in North America, the children of the flower children are staring into middle age, and the attitudes of American popular culture have moved much further into the world than they once did. Even back in the day, the evidence from the game I played could only have been considered *anecdotal*.

Still, back then, every North American I asked, when they heard or thought of *a rolling stone gathers no moss*, understood the *stone* as the positive element in the phrase, bravely rolling into some unknown future, freeing itself from that sticky *moss*. And everyone else, even most of the Australians, understood that the *moss* was the positive element. The poor *stone* was to be pitied, never having the chance to collect any of that good *moss* that grows around home.

Two for Francie Cuthbert

1.

Why Great Lakes Fishermen Shoot Cormorants

When they fly down trout streams
they are shot
on the wing

these greedy insatiable
fish-swallowers

their necks like snakes
in the water

they shit acid and kill
the very trees
they roost in

and no one ever speaks
about their emerald-green eyes

2.

Plovers at the Mouth of the Platte

After a very hot day in early August, I went up from the cottage I was
renting to the mouth of the Platte River at the south end of Sleeping Bear
Dunes National Lakeshore. Mostly, I just wanted to cool off, to find a place
on the edge of Lake Michigan where I could simply sit in the water and
watch the sun set. But I also hoped that I might get a glimpse of one of the
piping plovers that breed there.

The plovers are protected because they have almost died out along
the Great Lakes. They have the bad fortune of making their shallow,
exposed nests in the rocks and pebbles next to large sandy beaches, where
we also like to hang out for much of the summer, playing games, walking
our dogs, generally sinking into the glorious oblivion of summer by the
lake. There might not be room for both of us. During much of the early
summer, scientists—at least a few of them who think that perhaps we can

coexist—build exclusion pens around the plover nests, and volunteers regularly monitor each one. Signs along the beachfront try to educate all of us about the birds and about the efforts to save them.

I didn't expect to find any piping plovers. These birds begin their migrations earlier than others and have usually left by August or have gathered into flocks that pick bugs from the shoreline in more isolated sections of beach. Mostly I just wanted to cool off.

From the parking lot, I walked past the signs about the plovers, down along the bank of the Platte, where it cuts through the dunes in its last stretch before it arrives at the big lake. Even though the sun was setting into its August haze, it was still hot, probably somewhere in the low nineties, and the river was crowded with children drifting in the current. Near the mouth of the river, I crossed it, wading up to my waist in the cold water. I was already feeling better. The sun was setting, and I was surrounded by that glow that seems to exist only on the Great Lakes during summer evenings. Two boys, who may have escaped straight from a Norman Rockwell painting, were skipping stones out into the water.

I walked past them, heading south along the shore, glancing down occasionally in the vague hope that I might find a Petoskey stone or lifting my binoculars to look at a bird fly by. I had seen a couple of killdeer way down the beach, and I had tried to make them into the rare and endangered piping plovers. But they were too large, and they had double lines on their chests. They didn't have the bright orange legs I had seen in the bird books. I walked in the water, kicking along the gentle break of the waves, cooling off with every step.

I hadn't gone a hundred yards past the boys when I noticed a shorebird flying toward me. I got my binoculars on it and saw that it had a very light back and a white rump. I thought I remembered that mark from the field guides. I watched it fly by and up the shoreline, until it landed on the beach among a small group of five other birds that must have flown in behind me. I could see their dark eyes, their legs glowing orange in the light of the setting sun, and their small bright bills.

I caught my breath. There were probably fewer than two hundred piping plovers on the coastlines of all the Great Lakes, and now six of them were right in front of me. I didn't move but tried to steady my binoculars so I could get a good look at them.

And at that very moment the two cute little boys out doing their Huck Finn thing on a hot summer evening . . . threw stones at the plovers.

The birds fluttered up and away, none of them hurt. They flew out over the water, circled, and came back into the shore, clearly not overly frightened by the boys or their stones. I wanted to yell and wave my arms, but I was speechless. I started trudging toward the boys as quickly as I could.

Perhaps they had seen me watching the birds. Perhaps they were just a bit frightened by the sight of a sweaty Santa Claus coming straight for them through the sand. They turned up the beach and ran off, almost leaping through the river and back toward the parking lot. I saw that they talked to a man and a woman as they ran past.

I am not a person given to forcing his political views—even his environmental views—on strangers. Maybe I'll try to write about issues, or more likely simply try to describe things I find beautiful, but I never browbeat strangers. Still, I walked straight up to this couple and greeted them.

"Those birds, the ones the boys were throwing stones at, they are the ones on the sign. The plovers. The protected endangered species." I tried to sound informative rather than judgmental.

"Oh, they shouldn't be throwing stones!" the woman said. "We'll talk to them about that." Clearly these people weren't going to be defensive or belligerent about the whole affair. My resolve was weakening.

"Boys have to throw stones," I said. "That's OK. Just not at these birds." And the three of us smiled and nodded our heads. I started to head back for my car, but I felt the need to say something more. To make more of a point. Perhaps to preach a bit. "These birds are just too precious," I turned and added. "Too beautiful."

Now the man and woman looked at me a bit indulgently, clearly trying to humor the crazy old guy out on the beach who was worried about birds. I felt I had to say even more to convince them about the seriousness of it all.

"And if they'd killed one—God forbid—well, it would have been a $250,000 fine." Now they looked impressed. And they were suddenly looking at me as if I weren't quite so harmless.

I kept walking away, of course, but I'll admit that I almost felt like crying.

Therapy

The back lot behind my house was once a small vineyard, grapes neatly growing along metal lines connected to metal poles that were buried in three feet or more of concrete. I know because I had to dig them out.

The man who made this vineyard was an Italian Swiss immigrant. He built a small shed where he pressed and bottled his urban wine. I like to think of him filled with the memory of sun and the hope of wine, working quietly among his vines and under our relentlessly gray skies just a few feet away from his neighbors who were rushing off to work or catching the city buses.

After he died, college students planted marijuana here.

By the time I was able to buy the empty lot, the grapes had gone wild and volunteer redbuds, mulberry trees, box elders, and little wild cherry trees had taken over. It took me a week to knock down what was left of the wine shed. When I came home from work, I would grab a hammer and go at it, prying frames from windows or battering rotten board from board. It felt like therapy.

Things We Don't Know, Things We Do

My wife's maternal grandfather—we don't know his name, neither first nor last, because he wasn't married to the mother of his children, so he doesn't appear on any birth notice—died or was killed around September 1939, shortly after the Germans invaded Poland.

He was arrested because he had a wireless radio, maybe, or because he had a minor bureaucratic position in the provincial government.

He might have been executed. He might have been imprisoned or tortured, then sent home after he contracted pneumonia. Either way, he was probably dead before October and the Nazis had something to do with it. There's a chance that in his illness he might have lingered into the first months of 1940.

I didn't believe all this when I first married into the family. It seemed as if everyone from Eastern Europe wanted to transform their ancestors into minor heroes, unless, of course, they were major villains. Either you were killed, I thought, or you were complicit. I was wrong.

His mistress and his four children—ages two to nine—were kicked out of the house they could not inherit and began six years of wandering through Poland, Germany, and the war.

Before his death, he had transferred some small distant properties to her name. She kept the deeds and the rest of the paperwork in a briefcase.

The story—which I've heard only once—is that the mother and children were jumping on a train that was leaving the station. They might not have had tickets and might have been trying to sneak on an early train at the last minute. J, maybe eight or nine at the time, grabbed the railing with one hand. The briefcase, in her other hand, fell open, and they all watched while the papers that held whatever patrimony they would have fluttered behind as the train pulled out into the Polish morning.

That Room in Alberta

The last person who lived in the house my grandfather built in 1917 was a retired rodeo rider.

The place was isolated in 1917 and was even more isolated in 1997, when I returned. The road was hard to find. The house was a couple hundred yards off the road, hidden by a thick row of cottonwood trees my grandfather planted as a windbreak after he finished the building.

The old guy who rented the place was twisted and misshapen by a hard life riding bucking broncos. He walked with two sticks.

On a sawhorse in the middle of the living room—where my ancestors sat around an upright piano and sang hymns (I know, I have photographs)— was a hand-tooled, well-oiled saddle with silver studs. The old guy had won it at the Calgary Stampede sometime in the '50s. It had never been used and still smelled of fresh leather.

He couldn't climb to the second floor, but he let me go up the narrow, crumbling stairway. The two rooms up there had been abandoned for some time, maybe decades. In the larger room it hit me that this was the room where my mother was conceived.

She had died in Southern California almost twenty years before I visited the place and was buried down there.

To be in the room where your parents were conceived might not mean much to people with a longer cultural tradition in a particular place, but for a western Canadian, grandson of European homesteaders, this meant something, although I'm not sure what.

I went back to the place a few years later, and the agribusiness that now owns the land had torn the house down. They were probably afraid it would be used for a meth lab.

3

SOME THINGS LAST

God's Work in Alberta

My dad drove the Hillman Minx
from Kelowna to Spokane,
then came back up
the Radium Hot Springs road to Banff.

It was warm enough
in that first full week of summer,
but there was still snow on the washed-out road
between Revelstoke and Golden.

I was three weeks old
in a meat box on the back floor,
so we drove the long way,
my mother stoic in her pain,

because we were off to do God's Work
in Alberta, our family jubilant to receive
the Call, warmed by it even as the Hillman
wound its way between glaciers.

In Spite of Myself

When I walk into
the cabin up north
where I've stayed
for a week, a place
thousands of miles
from my father's grave,
a place where I work
with scientists studying
evolution and adaptation,
a subject he and I
couldn't talk about
without slicing
at each other, bitter
and certain of our ideas,
the first thing I smell—
individual, pungent
but not unpleasant—
is the distinctive scent
of my father's body.

Prayers from the Polish Church, Detroit, 1963

for Christine at sixty

Taken every morning from the Home for Girls
on St. Aubin to mass across the street
at St. Albertus where the nuns shushed you
when you snapped the hat clips on the back
of the wooden pews, you pulled down the kneeler
and prayed for the family in your unknown future.

After, the city and the suburbs,
Ann Arbor and that family dependent
on those prayers, half a century old,
that shaped even the travel, perhaps,
to that room above the harbor on Hydra
where you slept backward on the bed
to watch the fishing boats come in
quietly, guided by one faint bulb,

shaped, perhaps, even the redbuds
and goldenrod you cultivate now,
the new oaks you wrap with wire
to keep the rabbits off.

The Biblical Allotment

for my sister at seventy

We've known too many who haven't made
their three score and ten—what with cancers
and AIDS, bad hearts, bad drugs, and drink—
to complain too loudly of our aches and age.

It's all gravy now. More than we deserve
or should expect, all these moments among things
quick and shimmering in the light!

Jars of Air

A child of missionaries,
Howard traveled to places
the other kids at church
only prayed about,
but he brought back
jars of air.

He let us look deeply
into the sealed, empty jars.
We saw bits of pollution
drift past or tiny
translucent creatures
swimming through the air.

Evening, Late October

last to turn

hickories

yellow to terracotta

even close to dark
are illuminated
like holy women
in Rembrandt

from within

The Skateboard Park, Seen from Afar

Down past empty baseball diamonds,
the skateboarders glide silently through air,
their gossamer wings invisible.

Their wheels grinding against the ramp,
the crack of the boards
when they pop upward into flight—

it has all dissipated
in the space between us.
Even their mistakes are angelic.

Five Days After the Extinction Report

There's nothing one person can do

but because these things matter too,
when we find a least flycatcher
car-struck on an unpaved back county road,
a disheveled clump of feathers
but still breathing, Amanda, trained
in this art, cradles the bird, lighter
than a pen in her hands, warms it,
calms it, brings it back until it flutters
off to the swamp edge, calls once,
and is gone.

The Gleaners

(after Roethke and Millet)

For thirty years I've watched them stoop,
Fred and Ann, waist deep in green,
deadheading flowers
after their first blooming.

No wheat fields cleaned by hand this time
but the garden across Dexter Ave.
prepared at the cusp of summer
for its next extravagance.

They clip the plants below their seedpods
forcing a generosity of display that stops me,
for the pleasure and perfume of it,
all season long.

Infant Baptism

When she was six weeks old,
her mother exhausted, sleeping,
and me dumb and clumsy
in my fathering,

I wrapped her and took her out
one late December night
in a snowstorm
to see a snowy owl

perched
in a tree
like a gigantic, puffy, pure-white songbird
peering down on us,

yellow-eyed,
frightened or curious
or vaguely wondering if my daughter
might be food

when I lifted her toward him—
See? See?
Snow fell on her face
and she didn't cry.

Under Their Mortal Glory

I watched the old oaks
tossing in their mortal glory

while bits of dried bark and dead twigs
rained down on all of us below—

squirrels and chipmunks,
gold finches finished with their molt

and the small box in the corner
where Christine has planted

her first crop, her snow peas,
perhaps just a few days early.

Shadow Blue

Sure, you can call it lonely
out there along the unpaved roads
in the back corners of the county
on a Sunday afternoon in February.
A flock of horned larks picks
bits of salt or gravel kicked up
by snowplows.

It does look a little lonely.
Cornfields, grown bigger after harvest,
stretch up over low hills,
white and smooth under fresh snow
unbroken by deer or snowmobile.

So if you want to,
you can call it lonely.
But it's the best kind of loneliness—
when the late sun casts shadows
from maples or hedgerows,
blue shadows, but a blue
like no other, a blue without a name,
a dark, smoky blue
growing darker across the snow
as the sun falls.

Snow Light

Of course you can see it out of town
on an unpaved county road, but it's
obvious on Detroit side streets, too:

for a few minutes after sunset
on the first clear day after the first
significant winter storm when ice
crackles under foot or under tires,
and in that moment your whole world glows.

After the Holidays

Buried behind a thin layer
of clouds, the blue moon wanes
into another cold month.

The sacred days are over now.
Lent is weeks away. Still, light rises
all night long from snow
dusting the frozen ground.

Through the Friendly Silence of the Moon

I know that color—
moonlight reflecting off water,
white but not white,
water darker at the light.

We have no word for it.

I've heard there is a woman's name
that is that word, but northern tongues
can never seem to sound it right.

And then there is the ancient writer
who sailed his ships
through the friendly silence of the moon.

I've heard that sound that is not sound,
and I've seen the primrose
that blossoms in the night.

Let Them Be Left

(from Isle Royale)

What would the world be, once bereft
Of wet and wildness? Let them be left,
O let them be left, wildness and wet;
Long live the weeds and the wilderness yet.
—Gerard Manley Hopkins, "Inversnaid"

1.

Waves

North Superior
after a warm day

a short sudden wind
across the bay

riffles on the water
make long shadows

snakes of water
not yet waves

the lake looks confused
in that good way

just before the dance
begins

2.

Why I Try to Name the Things I See

That I can say "thrush"
rather than "bird"
and "Swainson's thrush"
rather than "thrush"

honors not Swainson
whoever he was—
possibly an estimable man—
but that particular bird

that particular thrush
who will live its life
out here at the end
of a lonely peninsula

on an island in a cold lake
and then migrate far away
not once caring about honor
or what name I give it.

3.

Going In

Wind caught my canoe,
twirled it,

and I went in.

Cold pushed my air out.

I gasped and splashed

toward shore,

toward the beautifully indifferent
spruce and cedar,
the wild iris and tiger lilies
blooming late
after their rainy spring.

4.

Bushwhacking

Scratches on both arms
and a gouge across my head

I feel better
than I've felt in months!

5.

Moose Antlers

glisten like bone
hold the sun
the brightest objects
on Scoville Point

nestled in a bowl
of basalt and blueberries
bone shed
after rituals of mating

eleven tines a side
the first polished
and sharpened to stab
and dominate

the bone-white palms
rivered with lines
of veins that once
fed the velvet

not a memory
of death this time
but bone shed
celebrating

in bone brightness
the spring-born calf
the generations
of moose

6.

Blackflies and Odonates

If I'm quick enough to swat a blackfly after it bites me, I find a smear of my own blood on my pants or my arm.

When two or three blackflies gather around the same bite, they seem more reluctant to leave and the bite gets painful. They are easier to kill then, but one usually escapes.

If the weather has been warm and the dragonfly larvae have emerged after their months in the water and climbed a reed or a bush then molted into their adult stage, the dragonflies (Order: *Odonata*) will swarm around me, picking off the blackflies that have come to feast.

Oh . . . the intimacies
of a life
among the bugs!

If a blackfly has taken a good meal from a protected spot under a strap on my sandal and tries to escape after I swat at it and soars up into the swarm of dragonflies, it will surely be snatched from the air:

Dragonflies drop the empty
desiccated husks of blackflies
onto the forest floor.

Dragonflies buzz over the lake
in their nervous
purposeful way

carrying a stolen spot
of my blood
to their dragon-crowded sky.

7.

Citizen Science

Canada jay, gray jay, camp robber, whiskey jack, *Perisoreus canadensis*, whatever we choose to call it, I find one, then two, out along the Point, late July, one adult feeding a fledged nearly grown juvenile

bobbing, jumping through spruce, quiet,
a patch of white on the head,

a splash of black on their necks,
shining gray under full sun,

and I enter them on the list, two more
data points to prove some things last.

8.

From the Bluff

On warm days seen from the bluff
down across the bay and the islands

everything's blue with delicate bands
of green. Dragonflies swoop in.

Gulls call. Loons float past.
I wait for the eagle to dive to water

and stretch its talons in to grab a fish
then roost above the nearest island.

Here alone in all this space
I cannot believe our world is dying.

4

BOTANISTS IN LOVE

Condoms, Abandoned on the Park Bench

I prefer to imagine the fucking
here last night was fantastic,
a perfect diamond to hold in memory

as their world turns bleak:
that night, last night, just a bit too cool
to be naked outdoors,

when they threw
their heads back
and whispered to the stars

while below them
the cars on North Maple
sped off to ecstatic destinations.

Time Before the Green Haze

Our yard gets bigger when the leaves
break out. The neighbor's house
shrinks and starts to disappear.

For that week or two before, twigs, thicker,
about to bud, cloak the lights
from down the block. The dogs
that barked all winter long
grow muffled and irrelevant.

Consolation

Even with the constant
high-pitched ringing in my ears

a day arrives in May
when I hear wind through leaves

and recognize it
the difference

that the week before was wind
rattling empty branches

Dear Erie

Some folks like to say you're ugly,
what with all those old stories
about your burning rivers,
and the algal blooms, the microcystis,
that late summer green slime
slithering through waves
out in your western basin.
Those are people who prefer
sand or granite at the edges
of their big lakes, who see only
nuclear plants, abandoned car factories,
and the swamps lining your shores.

But my daughter and I spent
hours one morning just this last spring
walking a peninsular trail
over on your Canadian side,
counting the rarer migrants—water pipits,
prairie warblers, clay-colored sparrows—
under a light gray sky
and a steady fresh wind
rising up from your water
that was clean and cold,
covered with rafts of ducks
diving for mollusks and fish.

Many, many thanks, again and again,
Keith

On Beauty, Jackboots, and the Rain

Outside the window of my little cabin, the rain is pelting down. It's cold and gray. All the moisture has kept the bracken green, lush until the back end of August. Usually by this time this far north it has turned yellow and is drooping into autumn. The water is running in small rivers through the sand and down into Douglas Lake. It pounds on my roof, and I keep checking for leaks. Chipmunks are beating out rhythm in my walls.

For the last dozen years, I've come up here to the University of Michigan Biological Station, Bug Camp, to teach an English class we call Environmental Writing and Great Lakes Literature. Even though we seem to have little in common, I like the scientists I work with here; some of them have become my best friends. But I'm really here for this, the view out the window on a cold, gray day—and sometimes for the view on a cloudless day with a cerulean sky. I'm not ignoring the sound of jackboots marching through the streets of cities farther south, but it seems obvious to me that if I ignore this beauty, if I do nothing to honor it, then the jackboots have already won. Sometimes when I look out past the bracken, the white pines, and the aspen to the lake turned misty in the rain, I can almost believe that the planet has forgiven us.

The Numbers at Kitch-iti-kipi

Big Spring, Mirror of Heaven,
ten thousand gallons a minute
shoot up through sand, clear, pure,
forty-five degrees all year long.

Nothing we can do will earn it,
the largest spring on the Lake,
or the world, no one's sure.
We are made of this.

The blue pool's forty feet deep.
Lake trout and rainbows below us
look to be a yard long
swimming above the bottom.

Moss on cedars at the edge muffles
the noise our children try to make.

Three Springs

Up where forests have pushed
back through fences, belief
comes more easily, comes
sometimes, for us, despite
all our learning, even
as it comes for that man
we both love. Remember
the day he took us
away from the lake,
from the roads, far
into a valley, fern-covered
and filled with the high calls
of warblers ready to mate.
Remember and this might help
you when, shaking,
you stand outlined before
our window, drawing from its blank
chill what comfort you can
against the fear mounting at night.
He showed us the stream
overgrown in watercress,
kept fresh, he assured us,
even in the heart
of the harshest winter
by the three springs he led
us to. Water rising,
unbidden, always rising,
spreading in an arc of green.
Remember and this might help
you as it helps that man,
our friend, who knows more
than I know of fear's
hard presence. Remember this:
We pushed our hands into them,
down through water and sand
until we could bury our shoulders
in that pulse of cold water.

The Lavender Farm

I know a valley, a real place
between two lakes, partly hidden
among old dunes, grass-covered now
or gone to aspen and young white pine.

If you drive there before harvest
in late July, through hills,
a purple meadow will open
before you unexpectedly,

its royal rows of color
climbing to the edge of your road.
Bees, drunk with excess, turn
slowly through the blossoms.

Into the Hemlock Forest

We walk down the trail at the edge
of Carp Creek, almost to its mouth,
then wade across.

The bottom is sandy, comfortable,
nothing to worry about, and the water
cold against our calves.

When we rise up from the creek, we are
among the hemlocks under a thick canopy
that keeps the forest floor almost bare.

The place is dark, quiet, cool—
church or crypt or cave.
We are quiet here
and think we might stay a while.

The Roads to Córdoba

> *Although I know the roads,*
> *I'll never get to Córdoba.*
> —Federico García Lorca, "Rider's Song"

Although I know the roads—

just a mile to the highway
then the freeway and another
freeway, across two bridges
and snow already past
my waist, another highway

two-tracks dying out
in snowdrifts ten miles
north of the last town

snowy owls and gyrfalcons
white shadows descending
through long twilight
for voles or boreal chickadees

woodland caribou
between cedars and hemlocks
hunched under snow
like white monks
singing requiem—

I know where the roads
end, yet I'll arrive far
away, comfortable, warm.

Twenty-Three Nuns on Warren Road

Twenty-three nuns, all in white,
walk with vigor down Warren Road
on a muggy August afternoon.

They dodge or step over branches, even trees
lying in the road, downed by the storm
that blew through late last night.

Dark puddles in ditches or hidden
by the bushes that grow next to Warren Road
reflect twenty-three pure-white habits
marching past with purpose.

I don't know if they've given themselves
to unimaginable lives of service or contemplation
or have simply found refuge from bad families.

They neither talk nor laugh, but all smile—
all twenty-three nuns, all in white, smile
when I slow to a crawl on Warren Road
careful not to splash the puddles
onto their pure-white habits—and they wave
that gentle country wave, one hand raised
in slow motion, only a quick recognition
of my moment in their lives.
They don't break stride.

Botanists in Love

for Alison Varty and Shane Lishawa

God, I love a swamp and that
even after the mosquitoes hit.

Sagittaria latifolia she says
and he tries *Myrica gale.*

They shout their binomials,
besting each other, flirting,
maybe showing off, just a little,
for the old guy stuck in the middle.

When he asks for English—*arrowhead, sweetgale*—
they say *Common names are for common people.*

But he's a common man caught
between botanists in love, third person
in a canoe where there are things
happening more important than paddling.

Just a couple of years before
jobs and children and fatigue,
they hit swamp water and lift
out, over mats of yellow pond lilies
(*Nuphar variegata*) until all three
are flying through reeds and bushes,
high on love and botany.

ACKNOWLEDGMENTS

In March 2020, just as we all began the COVID-19 lockdown, Laura Kasischke sent an email around to a large group of her friends and former students. She said she would send out daily prompts for poems to keep our imaginations active in the time of isolation. I have never been a great believer in the efficacy of prompts, but Laura, once again, proved me wrong. Several of these poems were first drafted in response to Laura's prompts, and I am grateful for them.

In late 2021, Marc Sheehan found his copies of a monthly newsletter a group of us did for most of the 1980s. Jim Daniels, Ruby Hoy, David James, Elizabeth Kerlikowske, Stephen Leggett, Diane Raptosh, John Reinhard, John Repp, Lee Upton, Marc, and I sent in a poem each month (or so), and we got a copy of the newsletter in our mailboxes a couple of weeks later. This was long before the time of email groups. When I looked at the work Marc found, I recognized a few of my poems, had thankfully forgotten many of them, and found three that I thought might survive with a little more work. Two of those revised forty-year-old poems, "Three Springs" and "The Roads to Córdoba," seemed to be useful additions to this sequence.

Some of these poems and prose pieces first appeared in *The Ann Arbor Observer, The Bear River Review, The Canary, Detroit Literary Magazine, Diagram, Dunes Review, EKL Review* (India), *Escape Into Life, The Fiddlehead* (Canada), *Hanging Loose, Hobart, Interim, Michigan Quarterly Review*, Michigan State University Libraries Short Éditions, *Orange Quarterly, Peninsula Arts Magazine, Poetry Northwest, Public School Poetry, Quarterly West, Rock & Sling, Skyway Journal, Third Wednesday, Voices de la Luna, The Wayne Review*, and *Willow Review*.

"The Gleaners" was commissioned for the 2018 Theodore Roethke Memorial Calendar, published by the Roethke Home Museum and Saginaw Valley State University.

"Consolation" first appeared on the "Words for Resilience" website produced
    during the COVID-19 lockdown by the Center for Public Humanities at
    Oakland University.
"Dear Erie" was commissioned by Anne-Marie Ooman for a collection
    of love letters addressed to the Great Lakes that she presented to the
    International Joint Commission on the Great Lakes (IJC). It first
    appeared on the IJC's website.
"On Beauty, Jackboots, and the Rain" was written for *The Newsletter* of the
    University of Michigan Department of English.
"The Numbers at Kitch-iti-kipi" was written for the collection *Seiche Ways*,
    edited by Ari Mokdad and Anne-Marie Ooman and published as a
    fundraiser for F.L.O.W. (For Love of Water).
"Waves," the first section of the sequence "Let Them Be Left," was
    commissioned for the dance "Water Studies," choreographed by
    Ari Mokdad and Elizabeth Schmuhl, first performed on the lawn of
    the Detroit Institute for the Arts at Detroit Dance City Festival on
    August 24, 2019.
"Three Springs" was printed as a poster by the Office of the Poet Laureate of
    the Upper Peninsula for the Marquette (Michigan) Art Walk in 2022.
Although first published in Canada, "The Last Monarch" was written for
    the YouTube film *Plague Phase: Voices in Response to Ecological Decline*,
    done by the nonprofit Nature Change, produced and directed by Joe
    VanderMuelen, Anne-Marie Oomen, and Bronwyn Jones.

Some of the poems in the sequence "Let Them Be Left" first appeared on the
Isle Royale National Park Artist-in-Residence website.

One of these poems was printed in the chapbook *The Ancient Murrelet*
    (Alice Greene & Co., 2013).
A few of these poems and prose pieces were printed in the chapbook
    Fidelities (Alice Greene & Co., 2015).
A few of these poems were printed in the chapbook *Ecstatic Destinations*
    (Alice Greene & Co., 2018).
A longer version of the sequence "Let Them Be Left" appeared in the
    chapbook *Let Them Be Left* (Alice Greene & Co., 2021).

Some of these poems were written while the author had artist-in-residence
appointments at the University of Michigan Biological Station and Isle Royale
National Park.

ABOUT THE AUTHOR

Photo Credit: Doug Coomb

Keith Taylor worked as a bookseller for many years and taught writing at the University of Michigan. His poems and prose have been published widely, including twenty poetry collections and chapbooks. In 2022, Taylor was named A. L. Becker Collegiate Lecturer Emeritus and Lecturer IV Emeritus by the Regents of the University of Michigan.